The Tower of Babel

Gloria Clanin

Illustrations by
Lloyd R. Hight

Master
Books

First Printing: November 1996

Copyright © 1996. All rights reserved. Printed in the United States of America. No part of this book may be used or reproduced in any manner whatsoever without written permission of the publisher, except in the case of brief quotations in articles and reviews. For information write: Master Books, P.O. Box 727, Green Forest, AR 72638.

ISBN: 0-89051-214-0

Introduction

When we look around us we see people with different colored skin, and different culturals and languages. If we all descended from Adam and Eve, why are there so many variations?

In the beginning everyone *did* speak one language, and everyone looked pretty much the same. But something happened to change that! This is the story of what happened.

God blessed Noah and his sons, and said unto them, Be fruitful, and multiply, and replenish the earth.

Genesis 9:1

As Grandfather waited for his grandchildren to come over after school, he enjoyed the gentle sway of the porch swing. A cool breeze blew across the patio as he thought about the story he was about to tell. He loved this time of day when he would teach the children more of God and His Word. Just then the back door opened and out they ran. Grandfather had his Bible waiting, and he quickly opened it to Genesis. The children sat close to him, ready to hear today's tale. Grandfather smiled at them and began:

After the great Flood, God said that as families grew they were to spread out over all the earth. They were to continue spreading out until there were villages and cities everywhere.

Just as it was before the Flood, many of the people didn't want to do what God said. They wanted to do what *they* desired instead.

The whole earth was of one language and of one speech.
Genesis 11:1

Since everyone spoke the same language and could understand each other, they could work together on a common goal.

The people lived close together and often shopped at the same marketplace. The market was the gathering place to see friends, shop for supplies, and catch up on the latest news.

God had instructed the people to fill the earth with their descendants. Instead, they decided to disobey God and stay together. They might have been afraid to travel to areas where no humans were, or they could have been worried about food supplies or wild animals.

By disobeying God and not trusting Him to meet their needs, they depended on themselves for survival. Many of the people felt they needed a better place to live, so they packed up everything they had and began searching.

As they journeyed from the east, they found a plain in the land of Shinar; and they dwelt there.
Genesis 11:2

One day the travelers came over a hill and before them stretched a beautiful plain. It was watered by mighty rivers and looked like a wonderful place for crops and herds.

Everyone worked together to plan and lay out a great city. There was much joy among the people because this seemed like the perfect place to live.

Nimrod, Noah's grandson, began at once to plan the city with a great temple at its center. It would be the grandest temple the world had ever seen! Nimrod hated God and wanted all the people to turn away from Him. The temple would be at the heart of his plan to achieve this.

And they said to one another, Go to, let us make brick, and burn them thoroughly. And they had brick for stone, and slime had they for morter.

Genesis 11:3

Noah and his sons had taught the first generations born after the Flood many things. Much of the pre-Flood knowledge had been lost, but building skills had survived.

The work on the city and the temple went very well. It was hard work, and everyone wanted it done quickly. But, no one wanted it done quicker than Nimrod. His plans depended on the temple!

Nimrod was already turning the hearts of many away from God. The temple would be the center of his new religion and he would be its god.

Nimrod's every thought centered on defeating God. The temple would be a great tower that reached toward the stars. Nimrod pictured himself standing on top of the tower and watching the people below him bowing and cheering.

The heavens declare the glory of God.
Psalm 19:1

God's people looked at the stars in the night sky and were in awe of God's creation. They worshiped the One who had created them and not *what* He had created.

Before people had the Bible, God used the stars to tell the story of Jesus. They didn't know Jesus yet, but they knew God had promised He would send someone to save them.

Godly parents would point out to their children certain groups of stars that made a design called a constellation. There were 12 of them and each told a part of God's story.

God never leaves His people without hope. The story in the stars told everyone that God loved them and would care for them.

13

When they knew God, they glorified Him not as God, neither were thankful; but became vain in their imagination, and their foolish heart was darkened.

Romans 1:21

Nimrod had a different purpose for the stars. They were a big part of his plan to turn the people away from God so they would follow him.

Nimrod gave the constellations new meanings and appointed priests to help the people learn these meanings. He began telling them that the stars could even reveal their future.

As the city and tower neared completion, Nimrod and his followers became more powerful. Since they all spoke one language they could tell *everyone* about this new religion.

It is our job as Christians to tell others how wonderful God is. Let others know that we must worship God and *not* the things He created.

We will not hide them from their children, shewing to the generation to come the praises of the Lord, and his strength, and his wonderful works that he hath done.

Psalm 78:4

Noah's great-great-grandson Eber was not fooled by Nimrod. He had been taught by his father to honor and believe in God. Now he passed on to his family the things he had learned as a boy.

He told them how God had created the world out of nothing, and about the first people, Adam and Eve. He sadly shared about sin entering the world when Adam and Eve rebelled against God. God had said they could eat anything they wanted except the fruit of the tree of knowledge of good and evil — if they did they would die.

Satan tricked Eve into doubting God's word, so she ate the fruit and gave some to Adam. They did what they wanted instead of obeying God — that is called sin.

God, in love, promised to send a Redeemer to save the people from their sins. God's people eagerly awaited this Saviour.

Let us build us a city and a tower, whose top may reach unto heaven; and let us make us a name, lest we be scattered abroad upon the face of the whole earth.

Genesis 11:4

After the Flood, God had told Noah that the people were to populate the whole earth. Not only did the people stay close together instead of spreading out, but they mocked God by building a tower to worship the stars.

It hadn't been long since the great Flood had destroyed the surface of the earth, and all the people and land animals not inside the ark. They knew God had done this because of the people's rebellion against Him. You would think the people would have remembered a lesson like that! But, many of them listened to the voices of men instead of the all-knowing, all-wise God.

The influence of Satan hovered over the tower. The closer the tower came to completion, the more evil the people became. Terrible things began happening as more and more people followed Nimrod.

And the Lord said, Behold, the people is one, and they have all one language; and this they begin to do: and now nothing will be restrained from them, which they have imagined to do.

Genesis 11:6

The tower was nearly finished. The people looked at it with great pride. They had never seen anything like it before. It was huge and had a look of power about it. And to think they had built it with their own hands!

Nimrod had used the years it took to build the city and tower to his advantage. He and his priests had been busy turning more and more people away from God.

God *never* lies or does anything that would force people to love Him. God has given us a *free will* to love and obey Him or to sin and disobey. Those who love and trust in God are His own dear children.

Let us go down, and there confound their language, that they may not understand one another's speech.

Genesis 11:7

As the dedication ceremony began, the sky over the tower began to boil with black clouds. The people at the ceremony looked up with worried faces. They hadn't seen the clouds moving in.

Suddenly the sky seemed to explode as bolts of lightning ripped through the air towards the tower. The deafening claps of thunder had everyone covering their ears with their hands.

After a few minutes, when everyone could hear again, they looked at each other in shock. The only ones they could understand were members of their own families, all the rest were babbling in some strange language.

Confusion was everywhere. No one knew what to make of the change. Soon fights broke out and the people began to be afraid of each other. Everyone quickly hurried home because the streets were no longer a friendly place to be.

Therefore is the name of it called Babel; because the Lord did there confound the language of all the earth: and from thence did the Lord scatter them abroad upon the face of all the earth.

Genesis 11:9

Since the people could no longer understand each other, work on the tower and city stopped. Soon family groups began leaving the area to find new places to live.

Eber's wife gave birth to Peleg just as they prepared to leave the city. It would be a new life for them, but they trusted God to guide their paths. They weren't sure where God would take them, but they knew wherever it was it would be a good place.

Nimrod stood on the top of the tower in a rage! His plans to become a god had failed and he could see streams of people leaving the city. All his well-thought-out plans hadn't done him any good.

No matter what plans men make, it is God who has the final say!

And God said, Let us make man in our image, after our likeness.
Genesis 1:26

As the families, sometimes called tribes and nations, scattered to all parts of the earth, they looked for just the right place to settle. Some families had special skills such as building, farming, herding, and metalworking.

As they traveled, they needed places to live while they looked an area over or built permanent homes. Sometimes they lived in tents, reed homes — even in caves.

Caves turned out to be the perfect solution for many families. They provided protection from the weather and wild animals. It must have worked well for some families, because they lived in them for many years. In fact, there are people still living in caves today.

Many people think that the tribes that lived in caves were primitive humans. That is a mistake because these "cavemen" were created in God's image, just like we were.

Seek the Lord . . . though he be not far from every one of us.

Acts 17:27

Other tribes and nations were more aggressive and soon had the best locations staked out for themselves. It would take a little while to plant fruit trees, establish herds, and gather building materials.

The tribe that settled Egypt is a good example of one of the more aggressive tribes. They soon had armies, began building cities, and used the Nile River for watering their crops. They quickly became a strong nation and began to build pyramids that looked a lot like the tower at Babel.

Everyone, before the confusion of languages, could write. But, now they needed to invent new written languages to match their new speech.

The tribes lived separately from each other, and married within their own tribe. Soon certain physical features became common in each tribe. After just a few generations the tribes began looking very different from each other. Even though they looked different, they were all the same race — the human race.

The Tower of Babel and You

Notes to parents and teachers — how to help your children understand the significance of the Tower of Babel and the salvation message.

We don't know what method God used to confuse languages — the Bible just says that He did (Genesis 11:9). The people had not *willingly* obeyed God so He made it impossible for them to live in harmony with each other.

As the families left the plain of Shinar to populate the earth they took all their possessions with them. They also took great knowledge and their religious beliefs. As they spread out and time passed, different regions of the world began to be dominated by different cultures and religions. Even though Nimrod was defeated in his attempt to rule the world, he planted seeds of rebellion against God that are the basis for most of the world religions.

Even though we look different, speak different languages, and worship differently, we are still part of the *same* family. Every person who has ever lived has descended from Adam and Eve — we are all related to each other! There is no room in God's world for bigotry! The Bible says that "God is no respecter of persons" (Acts 10:34). That means He doesn't value one person over another.

As the tribes spread over the earth, they took with them the sinful nature we *all* inherited from Adam and Eve. God is so perfect and wonderful He cannot allow sin in His presence. That's a pretty scary thing since the Bible says "all have sinned" (Romans 3:23). God loves you so much He wants everyone to have the chance to live with Him forever (2 Peter 3:9). He knew it would be impossible for us to *never* sin. Somehow our sin has to be taken away before we can live with God.

God had the perfect plan! He sent His own dear son, Jesus Christ, to pay for our sins. Jesus lived a *sinless* life and died for YOU! Jesus shed His blood on the cross so you could be saved from the judgment to come and live with God forever! Hebrews 9:22 tells us that "without shedding of blood is no remission [forgiveness]" of sin.

30

God wants you to have this *free* gift of salvation — but you must ask for it. Admit to yourself and to God that you have sinned, and ask His forgiveness. Then ask Jesus to come into your heart and be your Lord and Saviour.

If you have done this, you are now a member of God's family. God has given you His Holy Spirit to lead and guide you. Romans 8:14 says, "For as many as are led by the Spirit of God, they are the sons [and daughters] of God."

It is an awesome thing to be a child of God and a privilege to share His love and salvation with others. Tell your family and friends how they, too, can belong to Jesus Christ!

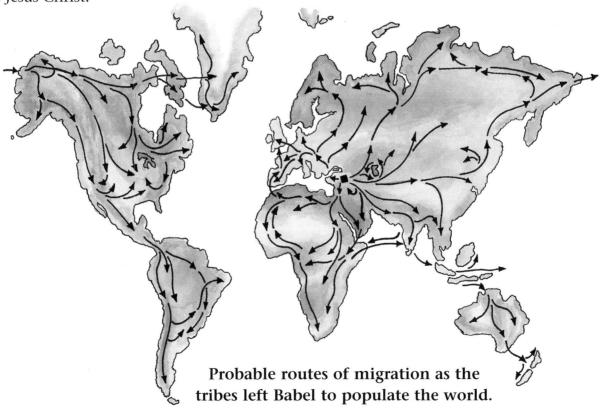

Probable routes of migration as the tribes left Babel to populate the world.

Suggested Reading List

Clanin, Gloria, *In the Days of Noah* (Green Forest, AR: Master Books, 1996), 80 p.

Clanin, Gloria, *Noah's Ark and the Great Flood* (Green Forest, AR: Master Books, 1996), 32 p.

Gish, Duane T., *Dinosaurs By Design* (Green Forest, AR: Master Books, 1992), 88 p.

Ham, Ken and Mally, *D is for Dinosaur* (Green Forest, AR: Master Books, 1991), 123 p.

Morris, John D., *Noah's Ark and the Ararat Adventure* (Green Forest, AR: Master Books, 1988), 64 p.

Morris, John D., and Ken Ham, *What Really Happened to the Dinosaurs?* (Green Forest, AR: Master Books, 1990), 32 p.

Oard, Michael and Beverly, *Life in the Great Ice Age* (Green Forest, AR: Master Books, 1993), 72 p.

Parker, Gary, *Dry Bones and Other Fossils* (Green Forest, AR: Master Books, 1995), 80 p.